The Mentality Changer

A journey to help change how you once thought about YOU.

Kyle A. Greene

Printed in the United States of America

First Printing, 2015

ISBN: 978-0-692-55948-2

Kyle A. Greene
PO Box 933
Blythewood, SC 29016

www.KyleAGreene.com

Dedication

Irene Green Gaston is not my biological mother in fact she was my grandmother. However, she carried me until God called her home in 2005. For twenty-three years she showed me what real unconditional love looked like. More importantly she showed me what real unconditional love felt like. I grew-up in a small town called Pineland that sits on the outskirts of Jasper County (South Carolina) but my grandmother calibrated my mindset in a way that made me think that I could go anywhere in this world if I never gave up. I had a very humble upbringing and my grandmother never allowed what I did not have to become an excuse for what I could not go out and get for myself. It use to hurt me seeing my grandmother cry at night knowing she did not have enough money to send me on a field trip because she had to either pay the light bill or buy her medicines, but yet I never went to bed hungry. This woman did not have a fortune but yet she could feed anyone that visited our house. Our four bedroom home was small (compared to houses today) but if anyone needed a place to rest their head she provided a comfortable pillow and a post. My grandmother knew how to always find the 1% of good in any bad situation and she had an uncanny way of being able to inject love when hate filled the air. She was like a superhero to me because I always wondered how she made a way out of no way so I called her my "Wonder Woman." She would always land on her feet no matter the height she fell from, so I called her my "Cat Woman". She could make pains disappear and problems go away so I called her my "Invisible Woman." I honestly do not believe that I would be the man that I am today had it not been for all the love and life lessons that my grandmother instilled in me. I owe absolutely everything to her and it is only right and fitting that I dedicate my first book to you grandma. Grandma, "Thank you! Thank you for loving me with no restrictions and thank you for believing in me when I did not even believe in myself." Let me end by saying something to you that you would always say to me, "I love you a bushel and a peck and a hug around the neck."

Table of Contents

The Journey Begins

Introduction

S uccess in life your life doesn't just happen. Every morning you wake-up you're given another opportunity to make it happen! Success is simply a mindset; those who 'think' that they can become successful many times DO. While those who think that they 'can't' many times DON'T. How are you thinking? How do you view your current situation? Is it a success or is it a failure? Are you basing your success on those around you and if so; who's to say that they're even successful. Quit looking into the mirrors of others trying to find a reflection of what your success should look like. Your success looks like YOU; you OWN your success. And if you stare off into your mirror long enough and you do not like what's reflecting back at you; only you   NOT your mother, your brother, your sister or your cousin but you have the ability to change it.

So do something in your life that has never been done. Do something with your life that will cause your haters to STOP and acknowledge your accomplishments. Achieve a goal that not even a family member said that you could do or had a chance of completing. Birth out that dream; the one that lives in the pits of your belly; birth it out into a world and make it one of   the greatest realities that mankind has ever seen. Yes you and NOT just me can do some amazing things if only you believe that you can. Yes you and not just others can defy all the odds stacked against you and you can beat back all the stereotypes to become whoever it is that you desire to be. Yes you and not just your favorite artist can one day drive your own dream car and you can own your own dream home. Yes you and not just the local businessman can one day own your own business, hiring your own people and being your own BOSS! Yes you and not just your teacher you can one day walk across that stage and receive your own PhD degree. You can do the unthinkable if only you think that you can. You can do the impossible only if you believe in the endless possibilities that surround you each and every day. And guess what YOU can reach heights that you once thought were unreachable but first you must reach out your hand.

This book was written with the hopes of helping you to change your mindset, change how you think about you, your success and your failures. I have seen too often people give up on their dreams when they're so close to making them a reality or people that blame their failures on others but lay claim to everything right when it comes to their successes. I know people who only see the bad in any situation never even making an attempt to find the silver-lining. I want people to begin to see the lesson in a loss, hope while facing despair, and love when faced with hate. If I

can help to change just one person then maybe that one person can then go on to change the world. Are you that one person that is ready to CHANGE your MINDSET so that you can go out and change the WORLD ...
#TheMentalityChanger

The Journey Begins...

Let me first start off by saying, "Thank you!" Thank you for joining me on this journey. This journey was designed with YOU in mind; the everyday hard working father, the single mom working, going to school and taking care the kids by herself, the young man struggling to figure out who he is, the student, the young adult deciding if it's too late to go back to school, the Corporate professional torn between starting their own business or continuing to help someone else build theirs, and the senior nearing retirement that is looking for some hope. This book was written to help shape or recalibrate your mindset. How have you been looking at your own life? Do you constantly allow negative situations to defeat you? Are your ready mentally to begin winning some of those battles?

Here are the RULES:
- The Mentality Changer was designed for you to read a chapter a day.
- Answer all the review questions at the end of each chapter.
- Reflect back on what you read and begin to apply the lesson to your life.

LET THE JOURNEY BEGIN!

Journey 1

Change Starts With You

C hange never starts until YOU first start to change. The single most powerful thing that you can change is your mindset.

Have you ever heard the saying, "No need to cry over spilled milk?" To the old me, that saying basically said this: there is no need to cry about your past because what has happened has already happened. You can't do anything about it; you will never be able to change those results. However, as I evolved as a person my mindset changed and I began to perceive that saying differently. With a changed mentality and a more profound way of thinking, situations that may have affected me in a negative way in my past no longer bother me in a way that gets me down in my present. Does that make sense? Understand this, nothing happens in your life without you first thinking about it; I don't care if that thought comes and then quickly goes in a split second. Your thoughts typically lead you to some type of reaction (good or bad) but one that you ultimately control. The sole purpose of me writing this book is to help you to change your mindset in the way you think and how you look at current situations. Something within me tells me that if I can just get you to change how you see your current situations and problems, then you can potentially change the outcome of future circumstances. Change doesn't happen until you make it happen!

It's funny because I can remember my grandmother always telling me, "Kyle when someone slaps you on the right cheek you should turn to the left." I would hear my pastor preach that same message in church but it didn't create the same change within me as it did when my grandmother said it to me. I applied many of the teachings that my grandmother (Irene) instilled in me and I know without a shadow of a doubt they have made all the difference in my way of thinking about life today. My grandmother was a woman who had nothing more than a middle school education but she was able to calibrate my mindset in a way that caused me to think differently about the things that happened around me. So in my teenage and college years when I would hear someone say, "No need to cry over spilled milk," I quickly jumped to say, "Who cares that the milk has spilled? The most important thing right now is to just clean up the mess." (Just like the mess that we sometimes get ourselves into and have such a hard time getting ourselves out. We lose focus on our mess never spending enough time cleaning it up and making sure we don't allow that same mess to happen in our lives again.) "You now have sole control in the outcome of the next glass of milk because YOU will now be in charge of pouring it; whereas, before you were not." (Just like in our lives when we allow someone else to be in charge of our future and as a result they shipwreck our lives and throw us off course. But, if you begin to focus more on you, this will allow you to charter a new course for your life--a course that will be more promising and fulfilling than your past.) Furthermore, I would say, "Whoever poured the first glass controlled how much or how little of the milk that you actually got. And who knows if they were not a hater that placed some poison in your glass with the intentions of harming you." (Just like the haters that we have in our lives today who hate on us because we are everything that they are NOT and we aspire to someday become even greater. Hating can be contagious, so please stay away from it and don't catch it.) In your life there is nothing greater than you being in control of your own outcome and success. It's funny now but back during my high school and college years I use to cheat off my classmates homework and test (not all but some) hoping to score higher than them on the same assignments or tests. Dumb right? We always ended up with the same answers so that meant we got the same results/outcome. Never did I realize (then) the stark reality that I was placing my fate and my outcome in the hands of someone else. Let me tell you something right now, only you--NOT your mother, NOT your brother, NOT your sister or your cousin but YOU--ultimately control the outcome of your success! Quit being so distracted and so enamored by the successes and failures of others that you lose focus of your own.

1. Have you ever found yourself in a situation where you didn't control any of the variables to the problem so you knew the outcome of that situation was already stacked against you?
2. What did you do as a result of that situation?
3. How did it make you feel? Helpless? Or inspired?
4. Do you believe that the outcome would have been different and possibly more in your favor had you been more in controlled of some aspects of the equation/problem?

I am not naïve because I recognize that in life we are not given (many times) a fair opportunity to control every single variable to the problems that we face in life. However, we must always control two key factors about our life: (1) our mindset and (2) knowledge. A banker one morning can foreclose on your house and a repo man one night can take away your car but no one will ever be able to take away your mindset and what you've learned in life. Equip yourself with enough knowledge to be able to fight any battle that may come before you because there are some mean and evil people that live amongst us in today's society who prey on people with weak mindsets and little knowledge. I strongly feel that if I can help to build up a stronger way of thinking (mindset) within you; you can then move yourself up and throughout the food chain in life. You can transition from poverty to middle class or from middle class to upper class. If I can get the middle or high school student who's being bullied to believe in himself or herself and to stand-up with confidence, I believe he or she can someday defeat that bully. Bullies are typically cowards that pick on others who are afraid to stand up for themselves. It is now time for us to break that chain and to inject confidence into our students. If I can get that person who has a billion dollar business dream to realize that what they have inside of them is greater when it comes out where it can one day impact the world, then that dreamer can change his life from the way he once knew it. But you must understand that nothing just happens or changes on its own; it first begins with you. You want to help change others; first help to change you! You want to help to change your community; first help to change your home! You want to change the work ethic at your job; first help to change yours! Other people are more susceptible to changing their ways once they see--NOT just hear what you do. We have all heard that cliché, "Actions speak louder than words." Let your actions speak loudly for you. When people begin to see your change be sure to let them know that your change happened when your first decided to change your mentality and mindset. We must begin this ripple effect throughout our families and our communities that will hopefully bleed into our society and cause a tsunami of change in the lives of everyone. You go and become the change that you once hoped for and help the world become the reality you once dreamed.

Big Sean currently has a song out that's called, "One Man Can Change the World." I believe he wrote this song because he saw how he overcame his struggles growing up in Detroit, Michigan to making it as a major artist that one day had the opportunity to perform in the White House. This song is to inspire both men and women that they do too have exactly what it takes to one day change the world. Maybe your change won't be as grand as an artist like Big Sean or Beyoncé or even like a great leader such as Dr. Martin Luther King Jr., or a charming politician such as JFK (John F. Kennedy) or like a savvy entrepreneur such as Steve Jobs or like an ingenious movie producer such as Tyler Perry or even like an icon such as Oprah, but if you can affect change on your block, in your neighborhood, on the streets of your community, or in your city you too will leave a mark on society. When you were born, you were given a date and when you die you will be given another, but the single most important thing between those dates is that dash. Change your mindset of how you once viewed situations and begin to make your dash count. The world is depending on you and the work that you accomplish between your dates. So no more saying, "Why me?" and start saying, "Why not me!" Learn to see the lesson even when you lose and be brave enough to still yet dream even when defeat stares you down. And, if life ever knocks you down nine times, you be strong enough to get back up and fight ten!

1. On a scale of 1-10 (1 being most fragile 10 being very determined/focused) how is your mindset/mentality?
2. Did this chapter help increase it? If so, how?
3. What do you want your dash to say about you?

Don't be afraid to change because you fear change itself or maybe because you fear the unknown. Change for some may even cause one to feel uncomfortable. But, there will come a point in your life where change will be needed and not just wanted. Change may take you to unknown places that may have you amongst unknown people, but trust the process and one day your name will be known. Lastly, I train my two kids in basketball so whenever I introduce them to a new dribbling combination (for example I may tell them to wrap the ball behind their back, dribble in and then out, with a crossover and then a step back for a jump shot) to create separation from a defender in a one-on-one situation, they used to say, "Daddy this doesn't feel right," and the reason that it doesn't feel right is because it is something new; something that they had never tried before. However, over the years I have reconditioned their mindsets to believe that no one can stop them on or off the court. So when I place them in these uncomfortable situations, I scream out to them, "You have to get uncomfortable at times to become comfortable at all times on the court." Do not be afraid of getting uncomfortable in your current situation to someday become comfortable in your future success. The success that you truly desire can be found on the outskirts of your comfort zone, but it may cause you a little discomfort to obtain it.

Journey Reflections

Journey 2

LEAD to Love Endlessly and DREAM

Fear screams at you to follow the crowd yet faith whispers and tells you to lead it. You were uniquely created to stand out so stop trying to plainly fit in.

For the life of me I cannot fathom why people like following the crowd. I do not understand why someone has the desire to be like somebody else. These days, I have a hard time wrapping my mind around the notion of people feeling the need to fit in when they were uniquely created to stand out. Just think, since birth (twins or not) you came into an unknown world alone but already with a predetermined destiny over your life. You were born in this moment of time to fulfill the purpose that was placed over your life, so quit trying to live someone else's. Knowing just a little bit about the human body, the one thing that you learn at an early age is that no two people have the same fingerprints. That scientific fact alone should tell us just how different but how special we are individually. But yet some of you for whatever reason(s) that I can't explain have been brainwashed by the media and wrongly influenced by your peers that being a carbon copy of someone else is cool. Some have been tricked into thinking that being a face in the crowd is cooler than being the face of the crowd. Many people believe that it's taboo to be different or to travel a path less taken in life by others. But I wrote this book to tell you or maybe even to remind you that in a world full of copy cats you should be the absolute best version of yourself. Let people see the path that you created and built for yourself and say, "He went against the status quo and made it!" Or, "She didn't conform to what reality TV portrayed for ladies and reached success." Walking a day in my shoes is hard enough, so I do not have the energy nor do I have the patience to try and walk a day in someone else's too.

As a kid, I remember a commercial that Gatorade created and it said, "Like Mike, if I could be like Mike. Be like Mike. If I could be like Mike." And it implied (to me) that if I drank Gatorade because Michael Jordan did then maybe one day I too could fly through the air and do things on the court like Mike (MJ). But, early on in my basketball career I discovered that that would not be the case because I used to drink a whole lot of Gatorade before, after, and during practices and his skills never became my skills. Actually, to date no other Michael Jordan has been created because a person drank Gatorade--yet we believed it was possible. Some of you in your lives right now need to realize that you (like me) will not be the next Michael Jordan or the next Tiger Woods or the next Sam Smith or the next Tom Brady or the next Lil Wayne, Beyoncé, Katie Perry, etc. No, you were matchlessly created to be the first.........YOU! Yes, you were carefully and preciously created to not be a duplication of anyone else but yourself. No other person in this world is as dope as YOU! No other human being is as outstanding as YOU! No other man or woman in the universe is as distinctively gifted as YOU! YOU, yes YOU were created to stand out not just to stand in. You were fashioned to be one of a kind not two of the same. You are like steal under fire bent, shaped, twisted, and formed to be the complete version of YOU. The world has tricked us into thinking that in order for us to be great or in order for us to be successful in life we must follow the crowd and to do what everyone else is doing. That way of thinking is absurd and almost offensive because it questions one's intellectually ability to think and operate on his or her own. I do believe in the old cliché, "If it's not broke don't fix it," but let me expand on it, "If it's not broke, don't fix it, but add you to it and make it better." People often tell me after hearing me speak, "Kyle you remind me of ET (ET the hip hop preacher). Are you trying to be the next ET?" And I take it as a compliment but I quickly tell them, "Thank you, but no I'm trying to be the first Kyle Greene," and they get it. They understand that I am trying to create a lane for my own brand and for my own success. I love to say in my speeches to students, "Why just ride the coattails of others when YOU can put the coat on and wear it for yourself?" I try to get students to realize that they can wear the coat of success or happiness and that they can make things happen in and for their lives only if they believe in themselves.

Be a trendsetter in your life, be a trendsetter in your community, and be a trendsetter in your family. Set trends and don't always be so quick to follow them. Allow people to see you do something that has never been done or even tried. You go out there and defy all the odds and beat back all the stereotypes because you choose to be different, but more importantly you choose to do it differently. If no one in your immediate family ever went to college; you be the first to not only go to college but to be the first to graduate from college. Maybe all your friends who grew up with you stayed in your hometown after graduating from high school, but you be the one to go out into the world and create a company that could one day provide employment and opportunities to those same friends. Let people see your lead and become inspired to follow it. Let people say, "Because he or she made it being himself, I CAN TOO MAKE IT BEING MYSELF!" Your life was never designed to follow the crowd. Since birth you came into this world to lead it! I need each of you to become your own author and I need you to write your own best seller for the world to read. Each of you reading this chapter has been destined for greatness in your own unique and very special way.

1. At this point in your life do you consider yourself a leader or a follower?
2. Have you been following the crowd or leading it?
3. What can you do right now to become the best YOU?
4. Do you believe that you were uniquely created?
5. My name is _____ and I am different because?
6. After reading this chapter, which do you desire: to be a leader or a follower? And why.

LEAD = Love Endlessly and DREAM!

Journey Reflections

Journey 3

The Go-Getter

B e a Go-Getter and join the 3% of people who make things happen in the world! Your time is NOW! You were destined to be great in this moment!

I often tell people that I am my biggest cheerleader when I accomplish a goal, but in the same breath, I am my biggest critic if I fail to complete a goal. However, I am not like the people on Wall Street that play the stock market game (which if you do, nothing's wrong with that). I do not get too high on my highs and I never get down too low on my lows. I have struck the right balance in finding a happy medium in my life. When the stock market crashed a few years ago, everyone who lived for the quick fix--just the highs--were hurt the most because they lost everything The people who lived for the lows felt vindicated because all they knew was what low felt like. However, people who were sound investors with a little business acumen were able to withstand the collapse of the markets because they were in a strong position in their financial lives. In your journey, you will discover three types of people: 1) The Good Talker, 2) The Go-Getter, and 3) The Bird Watcher. Let's briefly talk about each one.

The good talker will tell you everything that they want to do, everything that they are trying to do, everything that they haven't done, and everything that they wished to do. Some are very eloquent in their delivery and if you are not paying close attention to the results of their actions you will fall victim to the action of their words. The good talker simply talks the talk without ever having any intentions of walking the walk. And, if you are not careful, the good talker will talk you out of your dreams because you be-come so focused on hearing them talk. Good talkers make good associates that you deal with from a distance because the moment you allow them into your "friend zone" is the moment you allow someone who could potentially tear down what you have been trying to build up. They don't understand what I was taught early in life that "iron sharp-ens iron" and quickly they will begin to dull everything that you have sharpened because all of their talking quickly becomes a distraction to you. This type of person is good at entertaining you with their ideas but bad at helping you execute your dreams and/or goals. These people can come in the shape of friends, employees, or even family members and that is why you must learn how to sometimes love them from afar as they have the ability to hurt you the most.

Now, on the other end, you have the second type of per-son I coined as the Go-getter. The go-getter is the person who talks a good game, but more importantly the go-getter plans an even better one. The go-getter will tell you what they're after and then show you how to go after it. They will give you a plan of action on how to get from A to Z and then they'll show you the action of just how to get there. They will tell you that they have a dream and then over time you will see how their dream will become the world's reality. This type of person is a leader in their respective professions and people take their ideas and advice very seriously. Go-getters run the world as Presidents, CEO's, mega stars, and community leaders just to name a few. They understand that in order to get to the next level of greatness in their life they have to migrate toward other go-getters to push them even higher. In other words, they attach themselves to a mentor. A mentor (to me) is basically a person who you see as your big sister or big brother. A mentor will protect you from pitfalls or failures that they may have experienced along their quest to success. They share information that will make you a better person, they give constructive criticism (tough love), and they cheer you when you finally get it. A mentor can be absolutely essential in your pursuit for SUCCESS.

1. Do you have a mentor?
2. Are you a Good Talker or a Go-getter?

A go-getter never settles with being average especially when they know that they can reach something good. They never get content with good enough because they realize that they were destined to discover their GREATNESS. A go-getter will never allow fear to pickpocket them of potential opportunities because they understand that opportunities are never lost, they're simply passed to the next willing person who sees the advantage in the opportunity. I repeat that line throughout this book because I get fed up with those who miss their opportunities and then hate on a person who took advantage of theirs. Quit allowing fear and other people to hijack, rob, and take your opportunities to do something great in and for your life.

Finally, or, are you The Bird Watcher? A bird watcher is the type person that sits and yet watches from the power lines, or maybe from the branches, or even the sidelines offering advice or opinions that they wouldn't take themselves. As they watch from a distance, (because they are never involved in the action) all you hear is their chirping. Never do you see their contributions. The bird watcher is the person in your life who is quick to give you an opinion about what you did wrong, but they are never willing to give you the facts to help make things right. See, these are people who will stand for nothing, but they are quick to fall for anything. I once had this type of person in my life and for the life of me I could not comprehend how he always had something to say about what I was doing, but yet he never had anything to show for what he was doing. I kept him around never realizing that he was hindering my growth because I felt like he was my friend. But, let me let you in on a little secret about friends (friends who don't mean you any good): sometimes you have to learn how to love these types of friends from a distance. The distance between goals becoming accomplishments can be found in that toxic friendship or maybe the distance between dreams becoming realities can be found in that poisonous friendship that you need to sever. Yet, there is hope for a bird watcher. What I have learned about people that just sit and watch is that if they ever become inspired by the actions of others, they can go out to duplicate what they saw. Duplication equals replication and if a person can re-create a successful process that they saw then just maybe they can create that same success in their own lives. But, that success ultimately depends on the person and their drive, motivation, inspiration, and their discipline. A bird watcher can decide to become a go-getter, but a go-getter will never decide to become a bird watcher or a good talker. Right now in your life, which are you?

Are you the person who has been doing the same thing in your life but yet expecting different results? If so, that's call insanity. There are many types of people in this world but I chose to highlight just three: the Good Talker, the Go-Getter, and the Bird Watcher. I used to always hear (and still do to this day) that 97% of the population is run by 3% of the population. What I took away from that stat is that there are not a whole lot of go-getters in today's society. A lot of people just talk the talk or they just watch and talk. So, at this moment in your life, as you stand at a crossroads, you must decide whether you will go get it (dreams, goals, success) with the 3% or will you stand idle, watch, and ultimately be controlled with the other 97%? At the end of the day, everyone is given the same 24 hours, the same 1,440 minutes, and the same 86,400 seconds to make a difference in and for their lives. The one thing that you will never get back or the one thing that you cannot recycle is time, so be sure to use is wisely. Do not be the person to live a life based on regrets--regret that you allowed opportunity after opportunity to pass you by and regret in the fact that you allowed fear to hijack your chances of walking into your greatness. If you feel like you have been a good talker for too long and you have talked about starting your own business, then I challenge you to buy your company's domain name TODAY! Or, maybe you have been a bird watcher and you have been watching everyone around you go back to school just to move up the corporate ladder ahead of you.

I challenge you to fill out an admissions form TODAY! Take a Timeout from allowing good talkers to talk you out your dreams and make you question your purpose in life because they gave up on theirs. I believe in your ultimate SUCCESS. I just now need for you to believe in yourself.

1. Right now are you a good talker, a go-getter or a bird watcher?
2. If you are a good talker or a bird watcher what are you willing to change right now to become a go-getter?
3. If you are a go-getter, what are you currently after? Please, don't just say "success" and not list some examples. (For example, I am trying to start my lawn care business, get my master's degree, or make an AAU basketball team.)
4. Do you value your time? What are you wasting your time on that you can cut out right now to help you reach your goals in life?

Journey Reflections

Journey 4

Grind > Struggle

Your GRIND should always exceed your STRUGGLE.

In a very loud and busy world, I stopped and listened as these words were downloaded into my subconscious thoughts; "Your GRIND should always exceed your STRUGGLE." Let me first begin by saying that while I may not be the most religious person in the world (heck I can't even quote ten scriptures in the Bible), I am very spiritual. I believe in God and I believe in the power of prayer among other things. I respect your beliefs and whoever you believe in. But on this day, it was only God that spoke to me saying very clearly, "Your grind should always exceed your struggle; that is to bless you as you have been obedient in blessing others with your words." Those words would be the first design out of my #KyleSpeaks quotes t-shirt line.

These shirts have been sold and worn all over the country; my shirts have visited places I only dreamed of going. Those words don't just speak to me but they speak and pull on the hearts of others who have gone through the STRUGGLE and only made it out because they got on their GRIND.

Anytime or anywhere that I speak, I love to share my story. I believe that we all have distinctive stories that we should one day share because they are designed and intended to help shape and impact people's lives. I struggled so much growing up for many reasons: not having a mother or father in the home, being raised by my wise elderly grand-mother (who lived on a fixed income), and having a child when I was only a child myself (16 years old)--just to name a few. So, that left me with no other choice in life but to get on my grind (unknowingly). I say, unknowingly because I really had no idea back then why I grind so hard on the football field, the basketball court, and most importantly the classroom. I knew my grandmother and my daughter were my reasons why in life, but I did not know my what at that moment. I knew why and who I was grinding for but I did not know what I was doing it for or what I was after. How many of you can relate to being in this posi-tion today that I once was in my life? Let me stop to say this right now, If you do not have a why in life--a person, a thing, or a situation that inspires, motivates, and pushes you towards greatness, then you need to figure that out. But, once you discover your why, please do not be like me and just go through life not sure of what you are after. Let your why guide you to your what and then allow what you're after to marry what your PURPOSE is in life. There is no greater feeling in the world than to discover what you were created to do and uniquely designed to accomplish here on earth. So you have to allow your grind to exceed your struggle and no longer can you allow your struggle(s) to become your excuse from getting on your grind.

I wanted to know the definition for grind so I went to Google (our best friend) for the answer. Grind is a verb and it means, "to reduce (something) to small particles or powder by crushing it." I was curious to see how the urban dictionary defined grind and it read, "your hustle, good work ethic, doing what you do." So for the sake of this discussion I will marry the two meanings for grind so you can feel it the same way I do. Grind: to reduce your struggle by crushing it with your hustle and a good work ethic. We all have something that we have struggled with; it's all a part of life, but don't allow your struggle to stop you; get on your grind. Two examples come to mind: example #1 maybe you got cut from varsity because you struggled with scoring the basketball. You believe that you play good defense, you try to make all the right passes and you are good at getting rebounds, but whenever you get the chance to hit an open shot, you routinely miss, you blow open layups, and you are not able to create your own shot. Those are your struggles, so do you stop right there and just give up basketball? Basketball: a sport that you fell in love with as a child. Or, do you get on your grind to prove to the coach that you are an asset to the team? At this moment you must choose which direction your life will have to take to get to the results that you desire. Oftentimes, this is the moment when people give up on their goals and they give up on their dreams. Think about this, Michael Jordan got cut because he wasn't good enough and it helped propel him to discover his greatness! Do not be afraid of being cut by your struggle(s) to discover that you were born to be great. Or maybe you can relate with example #2: you struggle with your weight and you struggle even more to get it off. You are constantly depressed so you eat whatever you want with no regards and no plan to lose any of the extra weight that you have gained. Little kids laugh many times when you walk by because they do not know any better, but it hurts. Friends who once hung out with you when you were smaller don't even call you anymore to invite you out and your kids give off this impression they're embarrassed by you in public so they shy away from being seen with you. At any of these points you are given two options: (1) do I continue to do the same thing expecting a different result (INSANITY) or (2) do I decide to make a change; a change that will improve my eating habits and help me to implement a daily or every other day workout routine. If you decide that option #2 is best for you then you have no choice but to let your grind exceed your weight struggle. The days in the gym you are working out with a purpose because you are committed to a healthy lifestyle and a new YOU! The gym now becomes your new bff (best friend forever) and late night snacks become replaced with getting a good night's sleep.

People who are successful or have a desire to drink from the cup of success, GRIND like crazy because they understand first-hand what the struggle both looked and felt like. Once you have struggled for so long in your life and you begin to taste success it quenches your thirst. No longer do you allow your struggle to hold you back and keep you in a complacent state of mind. Successful people obtain success because they are willing to grind for it when others are content with where they currently are or where they have been for so long. There is a disease that is out there and I want to try and help keep you from catching it. That disease is complacency. The major side effect of complacency is feeling satisfied with how things are and not wanting to grind to make things in and for your life better. However, if you desire not to catch this disease, you must constantly stay on your grind. One must also not look at their struggles as roadblocks but as stepping stones towards their success. I have struggled most of my life, but the one thing that I have that no one can ever take from me is the education that I got when I was on my grind.

1. Write down what you consider is your biggest struggle(s).
2. How do you plan for your GRIND to exceed your STRUGGLE(s)?
3. What does your success look like to you?
4. Are you willing to get on your grind to obtain the success you desire?

Remember, let your grind ALWAYS exceed you're struggle and quit allowing anyone, anything or any struggle that you have endured to define who you are. Be the one in your family to defy all the odds or be that friend to redefine who you were and how you overcame your struggles to claim SUCCESS.

Grind > Struggle

Journey Reflections

Grind > Struggle

5

Journey 5

Winning is a Mindset

L osing is not an option! WINNING is the ONLY OPTION!

As a kid growing up, I didn't have much, but that didn't matter because I never really knew what much was or looked like. Granted, I would go to my friends' houses and I could tell that they had more than what I had, but I knew that the dynamics of their environment was different than mine. But, the one area in life in which I felt that the playing field and the opportunities were even was sports. Where I grew up no one had access to one-on-one or group trainings and nobody was going off to elite camps to specialize their skills. My success in sports was never dictated by which side of the poverty line my family fell on or the highest level of education my grandmother had. Sports allowed me to control both my success and my failure. One of the most important things that I learned from sports I still apply to my life today and that is: sports are only 10% physical but 90% mental. In other words to be the best physically, you have to first be the best mentally.

Winning is a mindset. Those who think that they can, WILL! while those who think that they can't, WON'T! How are you thinking about your game of life? Do you think that you are winning? Or do you think that you are losing? Some people lose the game before the ball is even jumped or kicked off because they have a losing mentality. The one thing that I know about a losing mentality is that it infects your mind then spreads to the minds of others. All it takes is for one player to plant a seed of doubt or a seed of defeat into the minds of other players and it destroys the nucleus of a winning mentality. I do not want to hurt anyone's feelings by what I am about to say but I believe it needs to be said, "In life, you WIN or you LEARN!" Losing only happens when you give up and you give in, but learning from a loss only happens when you decide to give it your all and you make a commitment to go all in.

I volunteer as a coach for my son's recreation and AAU basketball teams and I can usually tell before a game what the outcome is going to be. The only reason that I am able to tell the outcome before the ball is even jumped is simple, I can see the demeanor of a team during warm-ups to know who has the mental advantage. Remember the statistic that I gave earlier, sports is ONLY 10% physical but 90% mental. Just think, Michael Jordan (yes, he's arguably one of if not the greatest basketball players of all time) was a beast. I don't mean a beast in its true definition; I metaphorically use beast to describe how his game was on the court. However, he just wasn't gifted talent-wise, he was a beast from a mental perspective and he knew how to also get his teammates mentally prepared with him. MJ, as we affectionately called him, always had that look in his eyes and that swagger in his walk. He understood that in every game he was not required to score 40 points because he had helped to prepare his team by building a mental toughness and a mental edge about themselves. Many teams today walk in the gym defeated because once they see their opponent they tell themselves, "we can't beat them." Can't is a word for the weak and the uninformed. I stopped using can't when I heard a preacher once say, "I CAN do all things through Christ who strengthens me." So even when I'm weak I still believe and trust that I am yet strong because mentally, I know something greater strengthens me. I challenge each of you that have read to this point to stop looking at your problems as if you were already defeated, but to start starring at your problems with the hunger and the passion to defeat anything that comes before you. Quit asking yourself, "Why me?" and start telling yourself, "Why not me!" Quit looking at your glass halfway empty and start looking at your glass halfway full. If it is really halfway empty, realize that ONLY YOU can fill it up! Your success is waiting for you to own it. Stop renting your success out to others. To get to a certain level of success in your life and one that makes you proud, you must first gain the mental fortitude/edge that neither your haters nor competitors have.

Today, I encourage you to cut those losers out of your life: the people who hate on you for what you're doing to better your conditions, who criticize you for constantly making moves for your well-being, and who constantly try to bring you down when they see you trying to get yourself out of the struggle. Those people are weak and they believe that just because they failed or lost in one part of their life, success or a bright future is not attainable. It's time for us to have an open-heart surgery so that we can begin bypassing any blockages in our lives. We allow people to do 1 of 3 things to us: (1) build us up, (2) allow us to remain the same, or (3) tear us down. I am at a point in my life (and you should be too) where I can only afford people in by life to build me up. I have had people who were content with their lives so they never pushed me physically or mentally and I had people in my life that were only around to tear down everything that I was trying to build up. Cut those losers out of your life and start running with some winners because you were born to WIN! Your life was destined for GREATNESS! Losing can never be the only option. Remember you learn and then you WIN! And then you duplicate this process over and over and over again. You do it so much that you exceed your goals beyond your wildest expectations.

Michael Jordan won big in basketball because his will to win was greater than his will to lose.

1. Have you been mentally tough in your past?
2. Are you playing the game of life the right way? (90% mental; 10% physical)
3. Do you build people up, allow them to remain the same, or tear them down?
4. How would you measure your mental toughness after reading this chapter? Do you believe you are in a better place mentally?

I believe it's now time for each of you to experience your "eye of the tiger" moment, where your will to win exceeds and overshadows your fear of losing.

Journey Reflections

Journey 6

A Champion Was Once a Contender

E very champion once started out as a lowly contender who did nothing more than trust his or her process. You have come too far in your life just to give up now.

The road to success is just that...a road. It's a journey filled with peaks and valleys, ups and downs, successes and failures, highs and lows. Growing up I constantly heard the saying, "Rome wasn't built in a day" and to me that simply meant that things cannot be rushed or sped up before it's time to mature and/or complete. It's kind of like baking a cake, and while I have never personally baked a cake myself, I always saw my grandmother do it. She would always buy the exact ingredients; she never needed measuring utensils (I guess she was just good like that); she always used her favorite mixing bowl; she would then bake the cake in her beloved cake pan and she always placed the stove on the same exact temperature every single time. She knew when to check the cake and when to tell us not to go into the kitchen for the fear that her pound cake might drop. It was like she had an internal clock in her head on how long it took the cake to bake completely through. The end results were always the same; family and friends closed their eyes and moaned out loud at how delicious her pound cakes were. She understood one key element in baking cakes: the process. She never got frustrated or even impatient during this process. Often times we find ourselves upset in the process because things don't happen instantly or when we expect it to happen. At that point people tend to give up, but when the going gets tough, the tough don't get to run or to give up, they get to go and stay the course. To do things the right way it takes time, good energy, a strong will power, a desire to win, and an understanding in knowing that everything isn't going to happen just because you want it to happen. Especially SUCCESS! Everyone wants to be successful in their lives but I am not sure if everyone is willing to endure the process that is required to obtain true success. But I write to remind you that a champion doesn't always start out as a champion; some champions started out as simply contenders.

I love to parallel realities of life with sports because since I was knee high to a duck all I've done is play sports. From my time on tiny mite's football to AAU, middle school, and high school basketball up to college football and track, I played sports at a very high level. Today, I now coach my son's recreational and AAU basketball teams because what I've discovered about sports is this: sports can be life's best teacher. When I am teaching my son or my players who I train the fundaments of how to shoot a basketball, I would say to them, "Be sure to hold your form and follow through. Always follow through even in life, because if you give someone your word they will hold you accountable for following through with it." I encourage my team to set goals, and I hold their feet to the fire in accomplishing them. I often remind my players what Kevin Durant once said when he was drafted, "hard work beats talent when talent fails to work hard." Then I would add, "So it doesn't matter how talented you are, you still have to work hard because someone not as talented as you are is working really hard with the hopes of one day passing you." I inspire my players to reach down deep inside when we're faced with adversity and even when defeat seems inevitable--to lose with grace. See, I have never won a state or national championship in any sport, but I have had the honor of coaching my son's AAU team to an NTBA (National Travel Basketball Association) National Championship. When we formed as a team, we were simply contenders with tons of potential and untapped talent that knew how to play basketball. As the season progressed and they began to understand the process and what it was going to take to be great, they bought into it. We not only won a few games or a couple tournaments, we won a lot of games and almost every tournament we entered. But then came Nationals, and at Nationals there are some of the best players and teams from all over the East coast. At this point I believed we were still contenders who had won a lot of games, but that this would be our ultimate test. I am proud to report that we passed the test and that we endured the process with flying colors as we were the last team standing on Sunday hoisting the NTBA National Championship trophy over our heads with the gold medallions draped around our necks. Trusting the process took us from a really good collection of talent to a really great and special team. Trusting the process took as from lowly contenders to National Champions!

The people in life who discover true success are the ones who first prepare for it and then, secondly, work really hard to acquire it. But after they acquire it, they stay hungry to maintain it. Some of you want to drink from the cup of success, but some of you are not prepared to do what it takes to achieve that level of success that you feel you desire. I try to instill a SUCCESS mindset into the kids that I coach and train. However, I do not want them to succeed in just basketball alone; I want them and I want YOU to succeed in life. I try to download this equation into their subconscious thoughts:

Your preparation+a good work ethic+ your gifts* your faith=
TRUE SUCCESS

Remember, success is simply a mindset; those who think that they can become successful many times do. Those who think that they can't many times don't? How are you thinking? Are you mentally prepared? Are you willing to work hard to make that dream brewing inside of you right now a reality? But, promise me one thing, don't be afraid of where you currently are in the process (your life's journey) because it's not important where you are; what's most important is that you are somewhere in the process. Do not be the person that fails to even try because you fear the process and the time that it might take to get there. A diamond is just not a diamond without going through a brutal process. Diamonds are made under intense heat and endure extreme pressure. Many of you right now are going through your "diamond process". Your child is acting out and being rebellious, you have more bills than money, your family has turned their backs on you, and you may even be currently between jobs. But yet, there remains hope as you have been burning the middle night oil on both ends trying to complete your master's degree, getting your child up for school every single morning, keeping food on your table, clothes on all your backs, and trying to keep the lights on all for the day in which you will walk across that stage to receive your master's degree. I encourage you to hold on and remain steadfast because your process will not fail you. Everything that you are doing with your life and for the betterment of your child will pay off in due time. How can I say that with so much confidence might you ask? Because I once was in that same position when I wanted to give up and throw in the towel. But then, I remember the outcome of my grandmother's pound cake. I remember how she sat there and waited patiently for the baking process to run its course. Then the parallel of the cake and the diamond came to mind and it reminded me that nothing great happens without a little bit of pressure and a whole lot of heat. The pressure in your life may be high and the heat may be hot, but your pound cake is almost baked and your diamond is almost ready to shine. Just trust your process because you are going from the valley as a lowly contender to the mountain top as an extraordinary CHAMPION!

1. What sports did you play growing up? What life lessons did you learn from that sport that you still apply in your personal life?
2. Right now in your life, are you a contender or are you a champion? (Remember there is nothing wrong with being a contender.)
3. If you are a contender, what are you doing right now to help yourself become a champion?
4. Are you currently under extreme pressure and intense heat in your life? After reading this chapter do you plan to push through?
5. When you become a champion, how do you plan to stay a champion (on top)?

Journey Reflections

Journey 7

Haters Sit Courtside

N ot everybody sitting courtside is really on your side.

Don't you think for a second that all your friends are really your true friends! Don't you think for a second that every family member who says they want to see you make it, mean it! Don't you think for a second that people in your church aren't praying for your downfall instead of your rise up! There are people in your life who show up every day to watch you play, and they are secretly rooting for you to lose as they openly cheer for you to win. Understand that these people come in all shapes, sizes, and forms; they may be disguised as friends who you assumed had your back, but who are constantly trying to stab you in the back, or they are a family member who wants to see you do good, but just not better than them. See, these people live amongst us with hidden agendas; their motives go against everything that they say. You can watch their actions but they tell a totally different story. Just think about that friend, you know the one who you continuously help out when they call you, but who is constantly MIA (missing in action) when you call on them. Please be careful of those people who prey on you but NEVER pray for you. People that prey on you seek to suck everything good out of you like hope, joy, life, and motivation while they attempt to fill you with despair, sadness, pessimism, and fear. Begin surrounding yourself with some prayer warriors--people who will always lift you up when others have let you down, they will encourage you to be the best representation of you and no one else, and they will breathe life into your dead situations.

As you travel down "your" road to success, you will cross paths with people who do NOT want to see you become more successful than they are. These people will secretly plot your fall from grace with the hopes that once you fall you will be too weak and even broken to ever rise or get back up again. But, in order to beat these type of people at their game, when you fall, try to land on your back. If you are able to still look up, it might serve as a reminder to get up. To beat these courtside haters and naysayers, you have to be mentally prepared and you must always remain strong sticking to the core of who you are as a person. These people – they will talk behind your back at night and then wake-up in the morning just to laugh with you in your face; don't become discouraged, you just keep fighting. You just continue to fight for your dreams, your goals, and your aspirations. You never let up on the gas as your drive towards the prize/the finish line because no one ever promised you an easy race. No one ever said that every day would be like Sunday or that every day would be sunshine filled. There will come moments in your life when the sun is not going to shine and isolated thunderstorms will seem to just rain over you, but be strong enough to stand even when you have to stand alone. Have the courage to fight even when it seems like you are an army of one fighting an army of a million. Have the resolve to start crawling when your running has turned into walking and you have nothing left in you but a slow crawl. Let those people sitting courtside who said amongst themselves that you couldn't weather the storms of life and that you would never make it; let them see you never give up in the face of adversity or tough times. Because understand this, tough times don't last always but TOUGH PEOPLE DO!

On your journey (whether it is to start your own business, get your Master's degree, or to become a better parent) to success you must understand that everyone sitting courtside are not cheering for you to win. Some of the same people who you assumed were on your side are really there to watch you lose. They only cheer when you're up because you're watching, but the moment that you fall down, they cheer even louder because you have fallen. That is why when you face minor setbacks in life, you stay mentally focused on the fact that maybe a setback is simply something or someone pulling you back to spring you ahead for your major comeback. I don't allow my failures to stop me from shining; I don't allow others who are too dull to sharpen my blade, and I refuse to allow anyone who throws shade to block the positive light that I try to give to the world. Never stop dreaming your dream! Never stop believing in your brand! Never stop striving for greatness! And never let anyone tell you what you can't do! If they are going to sit courtside and hate on you, give them something to really hate and to really talk about. Right now, if you are currently playing in this game called Life and you are looking around to gauge your haters in stands, I encourage you to go so hard at whatever it is that you do that you make your haters your cheerleaders. Be so committed to accomplishing something great in and for your life that you make the doubters your believers! Make the people who once said, "You will never amount to anything," have to mount up enough courage to apologize because you have super exceeded their expectations.

1. Have you ever experienced family or friends sitting courtside wishing for you to lose?
2. How did it make you feel? Did it make you want to give up?
3. Self-Assessment time, are you cheering for the people in your life to succeed or fail?

I simply ask that last question because often times we become that person who cheers for others to fail in their endeavors unknowingly because we feel threatened by their success. What I have experienced in my own life I want to share with you. If you work hard enough, if you stay disciplined enough, and if you give enough of yourself to your dreams and your goals, you will never have enough energy to hate on anyone else's success because you will be so focused on yours. Also, when you hate on others, you block your own blessings. So, if you can't figure out why things are not happening in your life, starting by removing the hate that you may have for someone else's success and see what happens with yours.

Now, go make your will to WIN greater than your fear to lose.

Journey Reflections

Journey 8

Triumph! Success! Victory!

Your TRIUMPH can be found on the other side of your tribulation; your SUCCESS can be seen on the other side of your failure; and your VICTORY can be won on the other side of your defeat. Trust the process and find your GOOD even in your bad.

Too many times we look at just our negatives (trials, tribulations, failures, and defeats) and think that we will never amount to anything in life. Yet not once do we see any of our positives (triumphs, wins, successes, and victories) and think that just maybe our life is on the right track. Some people look at a lost job and think that a better job is not possible, and they look at a failed relationship and stop holding onto hope for one day having a winning marriage. We allow negatives to keep us away from our potential positives, and if you live a life based on this perception, then you will never fully know what success feels like. If we look at some of the most successful people right in our time, their mentalities around this premise of success and failure are different for they understand that failures and defeats are simply a part of their success process. I once heard someone say, "Fail your way to success." I remember when I first heard that I wasn't in a place in my life to fully understand what it meant--not just to me but what it meant in general. I asked myself, "How can you fail your way to success? That's the dumbest thing I've ever heard." Have you ever asked yourself a similar question when you heard a successful person give advice that you didn't fully agree with because you didn't understand the mentality from which they spoke? Let me be the first to raise my hand; I was that person. But, as I began to slowly change my mentality and as my way of thinking evolved, only then is when that statement resonated within me. If I fail I get back up, I try again. If I fail again I get back up and I try again even harder. But, as long as I keep getting back up and never giving up, I give myself a chance. And in life, ladies and gentlemen, all you want is a chance. Whether, that chance is fair or not, all you need is for the world to give you one. One chance after all the failures you endured can produce the type of success that you once desired. Do NOT let a chance or an opportunity to discover success and to be great pass you by.

If you want to hear about a successful person who took their test and made it their TESTimony or took their mess and made it their MESSage, look at the story of Tyler Perry. Not only did he defy all the odds that Hollywood set before him; he confronted and then conquered all the odds that his peers, friends, and family members placed before him. Tyler Perry understood that as long as he believed in himself and a higher being and followed his dreams, success would no longer elude him. Mr. Perry stated in a video that he would go from city to city showing his plays (which we would one day come to love) with hardly anyone showing up to support him. He said (paraphrasing) he was homeless, living in his car, but yet believing in his dream, trusting in his God, and holding out hope that an opportunity/a chance would come for him to show the world his true writing and producing savvy. His chance came and he delivered! Now when Tyler Perry releases a new movie, we flock to theaters; when his plays come to our cities, we show up in droves; and when one of his TV sitcoms are aired, we are glued to our television sets eagerly watching. I believe that Tyler Perry would tell anyone that he is no different than any of us, but he knew that giving up on his dreams was never an option.

Have you given up on your dreams? If so, why? Which one of you reading this will have the next Tyler Perry story? Who reading this right now is ready to fight just a little bit harder and smarter? Everything that you have been through thus far in life has prepared you for this moment. Every trial isn't meant to persecute you; some are simply meant to prepare you for something greater in your life. Every failure is not intended for you to give up; sometimes the intentions behind the failure is to get you to give it just a little bit more. There is this very profound cartoon illustration floating around social media of two men with the same type of digging tool, digging through a tunnel of dirt. One man is only one dig away from discovering all the diamonds that are on the other side, but he gives up to just walk away. But the man above has more dirt between him and the diamonds to clear, but yet he's still digging. Of the two men, which are you? The one who's almost there for the prize/success but you walked away because you feel like you've been at it for so long? Or are you the man who is there in that tunnel still digging not worried about anything or anyone but the prize/success that awaits on the other side? On the other side of your heartbreak, pain, failures, losses, trials and tribulations, there lives love, hope, optimism, winning, victory, and success. In school I was always taught that two negatives equal a positive; so if you are currently experiencing (-) failure and (-) defeat in your life, don't give up, keep fighting because your results may one day surprise you as you fail your way to (+) SUCCESS.

1. How do you view the negatives in your life? For example, do failures depress you and make you want to give up on your dreams/goals?
2. Do you believe that you can fail your way to success?
3. What does that saying, "Fail your way to success" mean to you?
4. Which of the two digging men do your actions align with?
5. Are you ready to turn your negatives into some positives in the next chapter of your life?

Journey Reflections

Triumph! Success! Victory!

Journey 9

Live F.L.A.W.L.E.S.S.

"**I** woke up like this." No I actually fought hard for this!

I did NOT wake up like this. I was NOT even born like this. What you see now is NOT what it was always like. I am a flawed individual who is constantly working to make myself a better person. I am simply an imperfect vessel who is being used to carry out His perfect will here on Earth (I will never forget when a friend said something similar to me). No one is perfect and perfection is not attainable. However, we can make strides to live a life that is in line to His perfection. As human beings we will naturally fail in this quest for perfection, and we will even mistakes along the way, but be sure that the times that you fail, you learn and the moments that you fall you get back up! In this journey you may even get lost, but make it your purpose not to stay lost. You did NOT just wake up like this; you had to do some things along the way to get to where you are today. Quit short changing your process and allowing people to take for granted your triumphs. From everything that you overcame (a domestic violence relationship that almost took your life, drugs, the streets, an abusive parent, death, and so much more) and from all the things that have tested your will to live, has given you that testimony that you have today.

Beyoncé, whom I consider a musical genius and I like as an entertainer, did NOT intend for people to think that she wakes up every morning flawless; with her hair intact, make-up on fleek, and breathe smelling like peppermints. Beyoncé's journey to stardom happened like most people; it took a lot of hard work, a recalibration of her mindset, an unbelievable work ethic, much determination, and a will to succeed even when those around her gave up. I honestly believe that the overall theme in the song "Flawless" is to empower women to always feel good about who they are (even with flaws) and to believe in who they are as a person. Self-confidence starts from within and then people see how much confidence you have in yourself. Let's get over this hurdle together; EVERYONE has flaws. We can look into our own mirror and find a reflection or two of some things that we wish we could change. Typically, we want to change those flaws that we find in ourselves for one or two reasons: (1) We think it will enhance our outer beauty or (2) we think it will enhance the way people treat us. I personally, used to think going bald was a flaw or having freckles on my face was a flaw, but then I realized those things were beyond my control. Losing my hair and having freckles on my face are both hereditary--those are features that I cannot change. However, I can change my attitude, I can control my drive, I can alter my dedication, I can adjust to my failures, and I can pursue my ambitions vigorously. Don't simply be the one to just change your outer beauty and not change you inner beauty in the process. Some of the most beautiful people have some of the ugliest personalities. People, after time, may forget what you look like, but they will never forget how hard you worked or how good you made them feel.

I used to always hear, "He who is without sins, cast the first rock." But for the sake of this lesson remove sins and replace it with flaws: "He who is without flaws cast the first rock." I do not believe anyone can cast that rock first because we are all flawed individuals. Our flaws are like our fingerprints they are the things that uniquely separate us from one another, but our stories, our trials, our tribulations, our triumphs, and our successes are the things that connect us. Quit judging and even stereotyping people because their flaws look different than yours; learn to accept and love all people for who they are and what they do to make this world a better place. Stop allowing your flaws to handicap you from doing something great in life because you fear someone calling you out because of your flaw. Remember, no one wakes up FLAWLESS; we are all perfectly imperfect and beautifully flawed.

1. If you could change one external flaw about you what would it be and why?
2. If you could change one internal flaw about you what would it be and why?
3. Have you found yourself looking down on other people's flaws?

Live
F – Fearless
L – Loving
A – Ambitious
W – Winning
L – Limitless
E – Energetic
S – Successful
S – Surviving

So go out and be FLAWLESS in everything that you do!

Journey Reflections

Journey 10

You Can't Box Me In

When you die they (the world) will place you in a box; so do something special with your life right now that won't allow them to place you in one while you LIVE!

How many times has someone told you that you would never amount to anything? Or has anyone tried to tell you how you were going to live your life? Can you remember a time when people doubted your ability to think for yourself? Have people constantly tried to play your intelligence? Am I the only person that has had someone question my educated choices and decisions? Has a friend ever said, "I got you and I won't let anything happen to you" but they eventually happened to you and as a result of their toxic friendship they kept you from climbing to the next level in your life? Has anyone ever experienced a family member who has done nothing with their life and they are constantly trying to keep you boxed in from doing anything with yours? Can anyone else relate to these types of situations that I have personally experienced in my life alone?

I am almost certain that at some juncture in your life you have had people to try and put you in a box. Many times it is a box in which they have already placed themselves and have no earthly idea on how to get themselves out. They feel that since they are unable to free, release or escape their own imprisonment it is easier to box in others like family and friends. They do this because family and friends are typically the two biggest and most influential groups of people that are easily persuaded into this entrapment. Why is that? We humbly believe that our family and friends would never do anything to hurt us or to jeopardize our well-being. Well, let me stop right here and be honest with you; your family and friends (at times) are the ones that will hurt you first and they are the ones that will hurt you the most. Some will do it unknowingly, never realizing that they are hurting or hindering your growth in life. But there are others that will see their ship sinking and they will do everything in their power to ensure that your ship sinks in the process too. It is your job to stay away from those un-wanted anchors in your life because they specialize in hold-ing you down, pulling you down, and keeping you down from opportunities which can help take you higher in life. One of the hardest things for us to do from this point is moving past this family member or friend. Right now, you need to master, for the completion of this book, learning how to love people--friends and/or family members who mean you no good--from a distance. In college, I vaguely re-call a song (the artist I believe was from Houston) that had a hook which said, "Back back back back give me 50 feet." There are some people close to you right now who you need to tell, "Back back back back give me 50 feet because you are trying to tear down everything that I am trying to build up and I refuse to allow you or anyone to destroy the success that I am after!" Our destinies have already been determined but we have an active role in how it plays out; so quit allowing others to box you out of your purpose driven life.

Today, do a self-assessment and take a full inventory of your life. Determine if someone or something has placed you, your dreams, and your vision in a box. Begin to ask yourself tough questions: "Have I placed myself in a box because of fear? Have personal failures boxed me into thinking I am a failure? What was the defining moment that got me in this box? And, what will be the redefining moment that will get me out of this box?" Personally for me, I knowingly have allowed people to put me in a box. Never did I allow them to control me or how I thought, but they controlled my time. Time is a valuable resource that loses value once it passes you by because it becomes a moment in history that once was. Time can never be recycled and once it is gone, it's gone forever never to return in its same form. I used to manage an artist and as a manager you are always behind the scenes doing everything to lift/build the image of your artist in the eyes of others, especially their fans and music executives. I was OK with sacrificing myself, my time, and my career to help launch his. My redefining moment happened when a kid that I had never met died in a city that I had never visited. I felt compelled and also empowered to hold a rally in honor of Trayvon Martin because I felt like justice was not given a chance. I believed that nowhere in America could someone be killed and the culprit not be held responsible for it. I took a step that freed me from the box that I was in and that step propelled me to where I stand today--helping others to free themselves of things or people that have them enslaved. My artist came to that rally as a huge supporter for me, realizing that my purpose in life was not to be a manager to him but to be a voice and a light to others.

Many of you, like me may have realized that you have been in a box for too long and it is now time for you to get out. For those of you who have been in a box for years, today is a good start in freeing yourself from this entrapment. This box has become your crutch in life and you have been using it as an excuse to keep you from trying to do something great in your life. DO NOT WAIT ANOTHER DAY. FREE YOURSELF NOW! Live a life today that your tomorrow will thank you for.

1. Are you currently in a box?
2. Who placed you in it?
3. Why do you believe they placed you in this box?
4. Have you ever been in a box and had a redefining moment that helped you to get enough courage to get out the box? Please share how you overcame that box experience.
5. Have you been the one placing those around you in a box because of your own selfish motives?

I am not naive because I do realize that we can sometimes be the one to place boxes on other people. We keep dead relationships alive because we do not want our significant other that we invested so much time and energy with to go be with someone else. Or maybe, we have a best friend who has aspirations of one day being the next biggest movie star and it will require them moving to California. So, we plant seeds of fear into their dreams to keep them near us. Do

NOT be that person! I implore you to live outside the box because when we take our last breath, the world will place us in a box six feet underground. Do not live a life based on the terms or on the restrictions that others have placed on your life. You live your life based on your wildest dreams, your biggest goals, and your audacious aspirations.

You Can't Box Me In

Journey Reflections

You Can't Box Me In

Journey 11

Unlock Your Greatness

One of the most important things that you have in you is your potential to be great. Do not wait another day to tap into it.

People who unlock their potential unlock their dreams to the world. You say to both yourself and the world, "Take me and use me for the betterment of mankind." Your dreams can one day become other people's realities and they all were birthed from you. Just think, what if Steve Jobs' dream about Apple remained just a dream in his head; would the world ever have iPads and iPhones? Or, what if Tyler Perry's dream of a big trash talking grandmother that we affectionately call, "Madea" who always seemed to know exactly what to say to calm a storm just remained a dream? What if Michael Jordan gave up on his basketball dreams when he was cut in the tenth grade? Who would everyone want to be like if we didn't know a Mike existed? Just think, what if Thomas Edison's dream of creating an incandescent light bulb only went off in his head, and if he not shared it with the world, would we still be using candles? There are so many more what ifs that I could list but now I'm concerned about your what if. What if that dream in your heart became a dream deferred in your head? Those same dreams that speak to you can one day speak for you. And, they can speak for you in a way that you never dreamed. Your dreams can one day say to others, "this person is great because they created an invention, a product, or a service that made my life and others' lives just a little bit easier." See, when you unlock your potential you ultimately tap into your greatness; because, everyone created has a level of greatness that is waiting to be explored. You, then, graduate from constant hurt when dealing with failures to sustained excitement when you experience greatness. You also, advance to a higher mental state of thinking because, why me when things happen in your life becomes a WHY NOT ME! Every minor setback from that point in your life will be seen only as a major setup for something greater for your life. See, when you unlock your potential you become embolden, empowered, inspired, and motivated to take on and conquer all challengers. You knock out all short term goals and you begin to complete New Year's resolutions because no longer do you see the struggles as roadblocks, but you see all as stepping blocks to take you to the next level in your life.

Those who unlock their potential discover their gifts. Your gifts are the things (your ability to sing really nice, your dynamic nurturing personality, your great oratory skills, your strong leadership, or maybe your gifted athletic ability in sports) that have been placed inside of you which allows you to separate yourself from other people. Not everyone created was designed to be able to throw a football like Tom Brady or able to dunk a basketball like LeBron James. Maybe you have a way with words which allows you an uncanny but very effective way to reach kids who had given up on life. Your gifts were placed inside of you to both indirectly or directly impact a person's life and also so that you might leave your mark on society. If you have yet to unlock your potential, then you have only scratched the surface of your gift(s). All throughout middle school, high school and even in college I spoke occasionally at schoolwide functions and my friends thought I did well but I was always afraid to speak before a large group of people. I used to stand there and read my nicely typed speeches verbatim; I hardly ever looked up to fully engage my audience. But, one day my daughter helped me in unlocking my greatness--potential as a speaker--when she told me to give her my speech and to deliver it from the heart. She looked at me and said, "Daddy who knows your story better than you?" From that moment forward on my speeches would become more intimate and engaging to my audiences. I tapped into my potential of going from a good speaker to growing to become a great speaker. I now allow my gifts to help shape our future generation and the world. Some of you right now need to unlock your potential and use whatever gift that has been placed inside of you to make the world a better place. Because after unlocking your potential and putting your gifts to work, you can then begin to live a purpose driven life.

And to me, the single most important thing to discover in life is your PURPOSE; why were you created?

1. Have you tapped into your potential for greatness?
2. What are your gift(s)?
3. Have you been using your gift(s) to make the lives of others better?
4. What is your purpose in life?
5. Do you live a purpose driven life?

"**Purpose** (noun) the reason for which something is done or created or for which something exists." We are all here for a reason and I want each of you to understand that your life has a purpose. You were created to do something here on earth and you have only been allocated a certain amount of time to accomplish it. The day that you unlock your potential and tap into your greatness is the day you begin to life a Purpose-Driven Life. Do NOT take your purpose for granted and young people stop thinking you have to be an adult to start living in your purpose. Your purpose in life does not discriminate on your age, your race, your sex, your creed, your educational level, or your economic background. Your purpose deals directly with you and the calling for your life; unlock your potential and walk in your purpose today. When you walk in your purpose walking wrong is no longer an option! Losing is no longer an option! Defeat is no longer an option! Everything dealing with your life will become like a big jigsaw puzzle that would have finally come together. There is something to say about a person that knows what their purpose is in life because they no longer question themselves on why were they born for they understand the essence of why they were born in a time such as this. My purpose in writing this book is to help shape, inspire and motivate the next generation, to assist in helping to change people of my generation mindsets, and to spread hope, love and peace to others across this great country.

1. Now, what does a purpose driven life look like to you?
2. Are you working to discover what your purpose is in life?
3. Go out and make your life truly matter!

Journey Reflections

Journey 12

Your Life Has a PURPOSE

D eath causes one to look deeper into his or her purpose driven life. Why were you put on Earth?

I complained a good bit last night because I had to come in
early today and work late on a project. I soon heard that a
young lady who I've only known in passing through meet-
ings and hallways had killed herself on yesterday. I immediately asked myself, "Kyle what could you have done to
stop it?" But my mind is unable to answer back. Maybe it's
unable to answer back because it realizes that while it is
bold to want to reach out to help everybody, we as humans
are limited in our ability to pull that off. The reason that
this young lady took her own life I may never know but
the fact of the matter yet remains; you never know who's
going through what. Individually, we fight our own internal battles and we wrestle with our own daily struggles.
Many times these battles and struggles are not even known

to those closest to us because we harbor these emotions/ feelings/thoughts or try to keep them caged in our own internal hospital. In our hospital we find ourselves being both the patient and the doctor; a system from which no treatment gets properly administered. Do not be afraid to ask for help or to go out and seek help for whatever issues that you may be battling. Have you been here before? Have you ever had an internal issue that caused you to fight with yourself or caused you to even question your relevance in life?

1. Do you appreciate and value your life?
2. Are you dealing with any internal battles?
3. How are you fighting them?
4. Have you sought counsel or advice from others?

Understanding why you were created and why your life is so special at this moment of time is essential in helping you to never find yourself alone or in a dark place. I want you to know that your life has a PURPOSE and that you are here for a reason. Never take yourself or your life for granted because when the Creator of the Universe pulled out His canvas to paint you; He did it while staring into the mirror. If you do not take anything else from this book please take this, YOUR LIFE HAS A PURPOSE and it was beautifully crafted. However, we must quickly figure out that purpose because the world is waiting on exactly what you have to offer it. I used to watch YouTube videos on discovering your purpose and I even read Rick Warren's book Purpose Driven Life (which was phenomenal, by the way) but none of those things led me to my purpose. I discovered my purpose (which is to help other's discover their own personal greatness within through my words, my stories, and my love) in life when I began to focus on the things that I was most passionate about; helping kids in basketball, being a voice in my community, showing students how I overcame my struggles so they can see that it's possible for them to overcome theirs.

1. Have you ever thought about what your purpose in life is?
2. Do you know what it is?
3. Write it down.

Even with knowing what my purpose in life is, I could not help my fellow co-worker, but hopefully I am able to help others along the way. I said that to say this, you too will not be able to save or touch everyone, but you touch and save the ones whom you can. Also, never discount a person's story or their struggle(s) in life because you have no idea how hard or for how long they've been fighting it. I challenge you here today to follow my lead in trying to live a life of service. I serve in three simple principles: (1) Serve those who are less fortunate than me. (2) Help those who cannot help themselves. (3) Remember always that to receive a blessing, I need to go out and be a blessing. There is no greater feeling in this world to me than to serve someone else and to help make a difference in their lives. I believe if the world got back to these principles or even began to adopt them, a lot of the senseless acts of violence would decrease and love would replace all the hate. It is now time for YOU to go out and be a BLESSING!

1. Do you serve others?
2. How do you serve others?
3. Why do you personally believe it is important (or not) to serve other people?

Journey Reflections

Journey 13

When Life Bends Expect a Break-Through

Your branches in life may bend but a bend does not mean that you or they are broken. Stand strong and keep the courage to remain standing even in difficult moments.

Have you ever come to a crossroad in your life when it was finally time to ask yourself the tough questions? Questions like, "Why was I even created in the first place? What is my purpose? If I died today would anyone miss me?" Have you ever felt like your life should be at a different level than where it currently is? Is everyone around you getting married and having babies but you seem to constantly pick bad guys who make bad relationships? Well, let me be the first to say, "You are not alone." Everyone has been there before and they too faced a crossroads in their life. Deciding the direction which you will take is important to your future success or failure.

One day I had become one with nature (not sure in what capacity) and I saw a little ole squirrel at the core of a massive oak tree which had come to a crossroads in its life. I stood peering out a window at my old job's breakroom, heating up some leftover spaghetti, when out the corner of my eyes the movement of a little squirrel captured my attention. This encounter in real-time lasted probably all of 60 seconds but as I became one with nature it seemed as though it lasted for 60 minutes. A squirrel quickly darted from the belly of the tree and made its way down one of the branches of the big oak tree. It would slow down to stand on its back legs before proceeding down the long branch of the oak tree. As it got closer to the smaller portion of the branch it seemed to have slowed down more and took more time in assessing the situation that was before it. All along, I had no idea what the end result of this squirrel's quest would be, but I watched almost in amazement as the branch slowly began to bend. The squirrel was keenly aware of its situation and proceeded with even more caution but precision as it made its way to the prize: an acorn. It reached down, grabbed the acorn, looked back to the center, and then quickly got back to the belly of the tree effortlessly. What happened next with that squirrel I have not a clue because I then started thinking metaphorically about how that squirrel encounter applied to my life and reminded me of how we as people come to crossroads in our lives and how we react to them. Do we have the courage like this little brave squirrel to go after our acorn (our prize/our success) or do we allow fear to rob us of our opportunities to reach our greatness?

There are four key factors in this illustration that we can apply somewhere in our lives: (1) the center of the oak tree, (2) the squirrel, (3) the branch, and (4) the acorn. The center of the oak tree is like our foundation, our core, and our strength--a place that we go to when times are tough. Our core is our belief system and the principles which we stand firm on and believe in. The squirrel is you; the squirrel is me. We are all like this little small squirrel where we are presented with a problem and we must figure out a solution that best solves our problem. In this example, the problem/the crossroads was how the squirrel could capture its prize/goal/success, the acorn, without breaking the limb and still make it back safely to the core of the tree. What is your goal? What are you after in your life? Are you afraid because your branches in life are bending? Be like this little but brave squirrel. Size up your challenge, slowly walk out on faith, grab hold of your success, and never forget to go back to your foundation (through prayer). The branch just like the acorn is very symbolic because it represents another meaning. The branch is your faith. When you finally decide to step out on your branch, you are saying to yourself, "I might not know if I can do it but, I am believing that there is something greater in and around me that will both hold and sustain me along this journey." How many of you have allowed fear to keep you from stepping out on that branch? Understand this very important concept: if you never step out on your branch (faith) you will never experience what it feels like to get your acorn (SUCCESS). Your acorn is waiting on you to come and get it. I am tired of people who say that they want to be successful but are too lazy to go after it. Your success in life is predicated on you actually doing something. Success doesn't happen through osmosis; it won't just happen without you fighting for it, working hard for it and being on your grind everyday single day for it.

There will come a moment where you will be at a cross-roads in your life, and you must decide the direction that you want to take for your life. I believe that if you step out on faith and you trust in something greater than yourself, you too will one day experience success. Quit letting a bending branch scare you or a failure stop you from going further with your dreams. The world is waiting on that dream, the one that has been itching you to get out of your brain for years. Do not allow another year, NO do not allow another day for your dream to go unattended. The first step to success is always the hardest, but it's always the most important.

1. Are you currently like this squirrel and your life is at a crossroad?
2. Write it down.
3. What are you doing to get to your acorn/success?
4. Have you stepped out onto your branch/have you tested your faith?
5. Are you like this brave squirrel?

Every day a squirrel wakes up and goes out to retrieve acorns. What makes you think that you don't have to wake up every day to go out into a world and retrieve your SUCCESS?

Journey Reflections

Journey 14

Trust the Process

Trust the process for your life and quit basing your success on those around you.

Have you ever (like me) at times looked down your timeline on Facebook just to see a friend from high school get a promotion on their job, or maybe you see a college classmate getting married or better yet you see a person that you have no idea how you became friends with them in the first place (but that's neither here nor there) post a picture of their brand new car. Your dream car! Have you ever found yourself wondering, "Why not me? Why can't I get married? Why do I have to go to this job where I am overworked, underpaid, and even underappreciated every single day?" Has anyone ever been at this point in their life when they felt like their process had failed them? To be clear on what "process" means I turned to my trusted friend... GOOGLE. Process in the form of a noun means, "A series of actions or steps taken in order to achieve a particular end." Process in the form of a verb means, "Perform a series of mechanical or chemical operations on (something) in order to change or preserve it." So allow me to dissect and then marry those two definitions; process from my perspective means, "Doing something in your life that will ultimately affect change for your life." Many times I come across people who want "stuff" (to be really good in basketball, get a really good job, to become a really good student or spouse etc.) in their lives but they are not willing to take the steps or to do the necessary things to help get them there.

I personally believe that there are three (3) reasons/factors that keep people from taking the necessary steps in their process to achieve the level of success that they desire. (1) Fear: fear is a bully that does not discriminate on a person's age, race, creed, religion or economic background. People typically fear the unknown or the fear of something new. Take for example, someone who wants to go from working in Corporate America to working for themselves. They are terrified of that jump. That fear leads us to number two. (2) Failure: no one likes to feel like they failed especially themselves. We can fail in a relationship and be hurt for a few days because we let our significant other down but that same person can beat themselves up for years if they ever let their own self down. Lastly, (3) What If?: what if I actually make it and acquire the type of success that I once only dreamed about. What if as a result of me becoming successful I have to lose some of my friends in the process? What if family members think that I have changed; how can I change back or am I supposed to change back? I believe these factors then contribute to you questioning, doubting and not believing in "your" process. And as a result of you not focusing nor trusting your own process you become distracted by the success of others.

When you begin to live a life always basing your success on the successes of others, you get trapped in the "Keeping up with the Jones" lifestyle which takes you away from your process. I have seen this lifestyle destroy people and marriages. This lifestyle has caused people to try and live (way) beyond their means because they begin to think like this: "I think I can afford a $300K home; Shannon has one. But my credit and income tells me that I should only try to afford a $150K home. Yet, knowing what the numbers show, I still will go out and buy the $300K home only to later foreclose on it." The foreclosure then affects your credit; your credit then affects your ability to buy anything else which then affects your marriage. Quit looking into the mirrors of others trying to find a reflection of what your life should look like. Your life looks like YOU! Your success looks like YOU! You will fail in life when you get away from your process because while we may want the same joys out of life, we may not have to endure the same struggles. PLEASE, understand that because if you don't know my story, you might not understand my glory. You see your friend from high school get promoted on his job, but don't know the hell that they went through job after job, year after year, to get this deserving promotion. But instead of not trusting his process, he stuck to it which in turn caused him to strive even harder to learn more skills for his new job which rewarded his due diligence and hard work with a promotion. You see a classmate from college post wedding pictures from her big day, but what you didn't see was the black eyes and broken ribs that she received from years of domestic violence. But instead of her staying in that situation, she decided to trust her process. So, she sought out help which helped her to change from the inside out, and she learned why it was vital that she learn how to first love God and then herself before she could love someone else. She trusted her process and it led her to the man of her dreams. Trust your process and wait on the man of your dreams.

1. Do you trust the process that was designed for your life?
2. Have you been basing your success on those around you?
3. If so, where has it gotten you?
4. Do you believe that greater success in or for your life awaits you if you begin to trust your process?

Remember, life is merely 10% of what happens to you and 90% of how you handle the "things" that happen to you. Failures...they happen! Letdowns...they happen! Disappointments...they happen! What are you willing to do in your process to ensure that when failures, letdowns, or disappointments happen you remain steadfast, focused and determined to achieve greatness in your life. For me personally, I trust my process, so I am willing to fight when others are ready to give up and take flight. I am also ready to stand for something when others fall so easily for anything.

What are you willing to stand for...?

Journey Reflections

Journey 15

Don't Be the Crab or the Barrel

W hen you make it up the ladder of success in life, don't forget to reach back and show someone else how to make it up theirs.

I was raised in the Low Country area of South Carolina and being from down there you either love seafood or you really love seafood. I loved nothing more than a good Low Country boil and what is a Low Country boil might you ask? A Low Country boil is simply nothing more than a combination of seafood and anything else that can boil together with it (ha ha). For my family and me one of the most important and key ingredients in this entire concoction is blue crabs. My mouth is actually now watering as I write this because I can eat crabs every single day of the week. Along with blue crabs, this boil can have shrimp, clams, mussels, eggs, potatoes, corn on the cob, and so much more. However, for the sake of this chapter, I just want to focus on the crab and the barrel to help illustrate their symbolism to our lives.

1. What does the "crab in the barrel" mentality mean to you?
2. Are you the crab or are you the barrel?

Growing up, before even knowing what having a "crab in the barrel" mentality was or what it meant, I would constantly see this type behavior play out among the crabs in the basket/barrel. It did not matter if we got all males, all females, or if we mixed it up getting both males and females together. Whatever combination which we bought, them their actions were always consistent. If one got up, the others tried and bring it back down. Just maybe they had an unknown pact from humans that they agreed upon which said, "If they take one, then we do everything in our power to pull the one up back down in the barrel." But as a kid and then as a teen, from my perspective, this is how I observed the crabs behavior: "When one crab makes it out the other crabs in the barrel will do whatever it takes to pull him back down." If I took that thought a bit further I would also say, "The crab that is so close to making it out has to worry about the haters doing everything imaginable to keep it from making it out of its current conditions/situations."

1. Have you had crabs lately in your life try to pull you down because they see you getting/making it out of your current condition or situation?
2. What do you do to ensure that you make it out not to return to that same barrel?

Let me be perfectly clear here, at this moment in your life, when you are almost out of the barrel that has keep you in bondage mentally, physically or emotionally, you have only one viable option and that option is to make it and become somebody in spite of all the other crabs that want to keep you down. These crabs come in the form of haters, nay-sayers, family and friends that do not want to see you do anything great in your life because they have not done anything great with their life. They become conditioned by the barrel which in most cases is their current environment or condition in life. For example, a person who has been born in the hood, raised in the hood, and who has never left the hood has a hard time processing how anyone that they grew up with could ever leave the hood. Please understand, the hood doesn't mean an area within a city that someone has classified as ghetto because a hood (to me) is simply a condition of one's mind about their surroundings. Just look at the early parts of my life; I grew up in a small poverty stricken town that was plagued by violence, drugs, and a poor educational system. Some could consider my home-town a hood or the ghetto but I thought differently and I saw my town another way. Don't make where you came from your barrel. Don't make the failures of others that are close to you your barrel. You be the one that makes it out and the one that defies all the odds to do something great with your life. Quit allowing crabs that are conditioned with a hood or a ghetto mentality to keep you in the bar-rel. It is time for you to breakout, step out, and to cross out everything and/or person that has been pulling you down in life. Cut the anchors of losers and grab a hold to those balloons of winners that are waiting to take you to the next level of your life.

But, please do me a favor when you make it out the barrel and make it to the next level in your life where you begin to experience sustained success. Do what crabs don't do. Make sure you reach back to help someone else overcome and escape their "crab in the barrel" imprisonment or situation. Way too often we (as people) make it up our ladder of success and instead of helping someone else make it up theirs, we sit and watch them suffer. I am NOT advocating giving people handouts. I am a proponent of giving people hand-ups in life. My grandmother raised me in the church (I make this perfectly known) so I would often hear my pastor say, "Give a man a fish and he eats for a day; but teach a man to fish and he eats for a lifetime." We have to get back in the spirit of teaching people how to fish because when we teach one; we reach one and when you reach one; you save many. If I can help to show one person how to make it, they can then show another and the other can help show the world. Remember, change doesn't happen until we first become the change that we desire to see. I challenge you right now to go out and CHANGE THE WORLD!

1. What are some things that you want to see changed in your life?
2. How do you plan to change them?
3. What are you willing to do to help someone up their ladder of success?
4. Can I count on you to help change the world?

Journey Reflections

Don't Be the Crab or the Barrel

Journey 16

Sow! Go! Grow!

The more you SOW, the higher you GO, and the higher you go, the more you GROW.

I believe that the more I SOW into others the higher I will GO in my own dreams, and the higher I go in my own dreams the more I will GROW as a person. Growth is an integral part in gauging your progress. When people fail to grow in life, they ultimately deprive themselves of any true and meaningful success. When I speak of true and meaningful success I do not speak of money, materialistic, or worldly things, but a success that only you can identify with. I have stopped basing my success on those around me, and every day that I'm blessed to breathe again, I fight for the success which I trust is best for me. And, as we walk in our true success, I accept as true that one of our moral responsibilities is to reach back and help others who may be less fortunate than we are. I do not believe in hand-outs, but I do believe and practice in giving HAND-UPS. If I see that you are down but you are trying and you are fighting to get ahead then nothing is wrong of me for wanting to help you with advice or knowledge that will help get you ahead in life and not behind in the struggle. The only way that people will advance in this world is by those in need; accepting knowledge and learning from those who are advancing in it. I honestly would NOT be the man that I am today had it not been for the teachers, administrators, family/church members, and business owners who made it, but did not think it was robbery to reach back and share it with me. The IT was things like advice on what it would take to make it in a tough world, encouraging words when they thought I wanted to give up, knowledge around sound business principles, and the support behind my dreams when I had no idea how I was going to make them my reality. Those are the people who make waking up so much easier for me in the mornings. They believed in what I could become when I didn't even know that I should believe in myself. Because of this positive impact on my life, I now reach back and plant good seeds into lives of others who show glimmers of hope, potential, and greatness.

1. What kind of seeds are you planting into the lives of others?
2. As a result of the seeds that you are planting what kind of harvest are you expecting in return?

I will be the first to say that I am not a farmer by trade, nor can I educationally speak on what it takes to become a successful farmer. However, I know being a farmer is kind of like being a parent or a coach. They all must first plant a seed in the ground. The ground in this case is seen as both the ground itself and metaphorically speaking, ground, for the sake of this illustration is a person. A crop will never bring forth a harvest without a farmer planting a seed. Your child will never bare good fruits in life without you first planting good seeds into their life. I can only passionately speak from this vein as a parent because I have been blessed with two amazing kids. I wanted to create great kids, (FYI: we all think our kids are great but I am not naïve--I was once a child myself) so I planted the seeds of respect, discipline, manners, dreamer, believer, fighter, hard work, grind, focus, determination, love, peace, hope, and sports, just to name a few. Once I planted these seeds, I went back weekly or even daily and I watered them. When I felt like weeds (negative people, thoughts, or situations) crept into their lives, I made sure I was there to help remove them and keep my seeds safely planted on good fertile ground. Thus far, my planting of seeds in my children lives seems to have paid off. I have a high school senior who has excelled both in the classroom and on the basketball court. And, my son is one of the top young basketball players in the state and has straight A's in school. My kids are always willing to help their friends and others who may be less fortunate than themselves and they are very respectful to their elders.

Just as I, a parent who plants seeds into my children, a farmer plants good seeds into good ground and then expects a good harvest. A farmer only stays relevant if he understands that his success is not based on a single harvest but that success is based on his ability to plant, to nurture and to harvest again and again and again and again. Bad farmers are only concerned with their next harvest, while great farmers are concerned with the harvests of their children. Are you more concerned with early but minimal success or are you concerned about longevity with sustained success over the long run? We are all farmers in one aspect of our lives: you could be a parent, a coach, a teacher, an administrator, a leader, or anything else dealing with people because at some point you plant seeds. Who am I to say if the seed which you are planting is good or bad? When you deal with people you plant seeds. I would both encourage and challenge you to plant good seeds even if it is into bad ground. Your good seed in bad ground could one day produce good fruit. Ask me how I know? Because I once had a mentor that stood in my small town like a big oak tree who planted a seed of greatness in me that I did not know existed and was even attainable for my own life. Even in the tragic death of the honorable Senator Rev. Clementa Pinckney, I bare the good fruits of a seed that he planted into me--a lost tenth grader about to have a child. I say that to say this, do not simply look at the ground and think that it is too bad for you to plant a seed into it. You have absolutely no idea whose life your seed can one day indirectly impact if you just make the direct connection in a person's life. Remember, you REAP what you SOW!

1. Will you decide today to start sowing good seeds into good or bad ground?
2. If yes, what type of seeds do you intend to plant? For example, if you think there's too much hate in the world, start planting seeds of love and peace.
3. Who planted seeds in your life? Why were they so important in your life then? And why are they so important now?

Journey Reflections

Sow! Go! Grow!

Journey 17

Your Steps Have Been Ordered

B e just as brave and as strong in your last step as you were when you took your first step in your journey towards success.

Many times the hardest two steps to make are the very first one and the very last one. The first step is typically the hardest to take because of one big bad word that's spelled with only four little letters: FEAR. We as people allow fear to whisper in our subconscious minds, "No you can't do it. You're not good enough because your mother couldn't do it." Fear hijacks our hope, it duct tapes our faith, and it steals our inner joy. But, I refuse to allow the fear bully to pick on anyone else. After reading this book, the next time fear begins to whisper, "You can't," you stop it right there and scream, "I CAN! I WILL! NOW WATCH ME!" Then you take that first step and then you place your next foot ahead and your steps will be ordered because then you walk in faith not just by sight. Oftentimes, people are afraid to step out on something (an idea, a dream, a career change, opening a business) because they can't see it. For a bird to know that it can fly, it must first one day decide to jump off a ledge. It quickly discovers that it was given wings to flap, eyes to see, and an internal GPS to help it navigate its direction. Some of you right now need to go to your ledge; your ledge could be you trying to figure out if moving to another city works best for your career or deciding if you should go back to school for a Master's degree. And, at your ledge you need to take the first step and then take a leap of faith trusting that you too will be able to fly. Just like money when you die, you cannot take your dreams with you. Do not live a life with regrets or what ifs. Live a life knowing that you were bold, brave, and strong enough to overcome the fear of failures or rejections. Some of the best athletes are only known for their talents locally because at some point in their lives they had either allowed fear or failures to rob them of their opportunities to showcase their talents to the world. Take your first step so you can show the world who you are and what you have to offer to it.

The second hardest step to take is the last because many times people simply never get there. People, while on their journey, give up on themselves and as a result they give up on their family and ultimately they give up on their dreams. A dream that once had so much potential and promise becomes a dream deferred. You must understand, but more importantly accept that the race is never just given to the swiftest. No, it is given to the one who endures to the end. During your race you will meet people running on the same level with you but one day they might pass you. At that point, you must not give up on hope or your success. For your success may be just on the horizon. I celebrate other people's success because it shows me that my success is still possible. You see on Facebook someone posting about getting the keys to their new dream home and because you still live in an apartment, you beat yourself up, or you see on Instagram a friend from high school getting married, posting pictures, and now you cry yourself to sleep. Cut that out! Your reflection of a dream home or a dream wedding is not in your success mirror at the moment. You just got a promotion at your job and you are making $20K more, but you fail to see your success reflections because they don't look like those of others around you. Maybe you'll meet your dream husband within the year at a conference for Vice Presidents. Remember that you may have never been in this position if you never took that first step to go back to college to obtain your Master's degree. Ask yourself, "Am I just looking for instant success to keep up with the Jones's? Or am I looking for gradual and sustained success to keep up with me?" Your journey is a process and many times we do not trust the process. We want to bake a cake in the microwave because we think it is quicker, but we know that if we just placed it in the oven and allowed it to take its time it would come out almost perfectly. During this journey you will take many steps along the way and some steps may be harder than others but no steps are less important than the others. When you make it to the end and you are ready to cross the finish line, let the last step allow you to self-reflect on your journey. Remember your bad days and think about how to cherish the good days and draw inner motivation from how you were able to navigate through your storms. Every day won't be filled with sunshine and blue skies. So on the day that you walk across a stage to be the first person in your family to get a Master's degree, you do it with your head held high and your chest stuck out because you earned it.

I personally believe that our steps are ordered and that we were placed on Earth to figure them out. I believe that mistakes and failures are only a part of our process and that they are intended to help us in getting to where we are destined to go. I believe that people don't make it in life because they fail to even try. You are rewarded by your effort. No effort equals no reward. People always tell me, "Kyle, man, you are doing a great job in changing the community." I usually respond with, "I'm trying." I answer this way because I believe that as long as I'm trying, something is being done to change my community. Success in your life doesn't just happen (understand that)! Every morning that you wake-up, you are given another opportunity to make it happen (realize that)! Choose today to take the first step towards your success and right before you obtain it reflect back over your journey and what it took for you to get there.

1. Are you currently struggling to take your first step?
2. Have you allowed fear to stop you?
3. Write down how you view your success.
4. If you have already experienced some form of success, share what it felt like when you got there.

Journey Reflections

Your Steps Have Been Ordered

Bonus: Journey 18

Students: You Are the Future

S tudents, take ownership of your future success by what
you do in your present actions. Your ultimate success is
discovered when you tap into your greatness. So I dare
you right now to dream the BIGGEST dream...

Students, believe it or not but one day in the past your
parents too were...STUDENTS. Can you believe that? Well,
it is true. That is why at times you get mad because you
feel as though they're getting on you the most when actually they're trying to protect you more than anything. This
over-protection mainly happens as a result of them trying
to keep you from tripping over the same problems which
once tripped them up when they were students. No one
person has all the answers to life's toughest questions. As
parents we get this concept but we also get that we play a
part in the success of our children. Students quit believing
that in your very young world you have all the answers

or that you know more than your parents. Being a parent myself, my greatest fear is seeing my kids fail at the same situation(s) that I failed at when I was their age. I believe as parents we play a major part in several aspects of our kids' lives but it is our main role and responsibility to help our kids navigate through life's toughest challenges. However, students I believe that it is your role and responsibility to accept the leadership and guidance from your parents. They have been battle tested and they have the wounds to prove it. I understand that we all will make mistakes (both parents and students) in life and we will even get things wrong in the process, but my biggest gripe when it comes to students is how you dismiss the help of your parents. As a parent the greatest joy that our child can bring us is a smile, a smile simply says, "Thank you for always having my best interest at heart." My prayer and my goal is to see every student make it and that "it" can be whatever your heart desires. When a star blazes across the sky, my wish is for every student to drink from the cup of success. However, many students today seem to be content with life and they simply settle for the status quo. In a time such as this where we wonder if black lives, police lives, all lives, or even if student lives truly matter, settling with just how things are cannot be your only option! I not just dare you to dream the BIGGEST dream; I double dare you to do whatever it takes (legally and ethically) to make that biggest dream the world's greatest reality.

Students, it is now time for you to take ownership over your success. Quit thinking that success eludes you until adulthood; success can happen in and for your life right now. Success does not discriminate on you because of age, race, creed, religion and/or your current economic conditions. Tyler Perry was once broke, living in his car, going from city to city, showing his plays and hardly anyone showed up, but he believed in himself and he believed in his dreams. His dream of Madea is now the world's coolest and funniest grandma. All you need is an idea, a dream, some faith the size of a mustard seed, a tunnel vision focus, and a grind unmatched by anyone. But first, you must believe that your life can have the type of success that you see on television. The young people who you see on shows like Shark Tank or on the big screen at movie theaters are no different than any of you, they just answered the door when an opportunity knocked on it. Have you answered your door? Understand this, opportunities are never lost, they are simply passed to the next willing person who sees the advantage in the opportunity. How many opportunities have you allowed to pass you by because you didn't think someone your age could accomplish it? There is a student reading this right now who could hold the key to unlocking the mystery of curing cancer, or maybe there is a student reading this who will come out with the next hottest social media website/app. You can take your dream and make it a reality for the world and your reality to the world can bring you a fortune. But, you must take ownership in your success and not leave your success to chance. So, if your future success requires you to spend more time studying in your present, then so be it; put the cellphone down for two hours and do something in your present that your future will thank you for. If you want to be the next greatest basketball player to ever play the game, then get off the Xbox and go work on your basketball skills for the next few hours. Greatness in your life will never happen if you constantly hang out with mediocrity and contentment. You have to begin to hold yourself accountable for the successes and even the failures that may happen in your life. Students, quit blaming everyone else around you (from your teachers to your parents) when things go wrong in your life because many times you going wrong will lead you right. Ask me how I know...because there have been moments in my life when I did the wrong thing and I suffered the consequences. However, those same consequences taught me a valuable lesson in what NOT to do the next time and it led me to the right path--the path less traveled. I challenge each and every student or young person reading this chapter to try taking the path less traveled by your peers and watch the difference that it will make in your life. Quit following the crowd and simply trying to fit in when deep down inside you know that you want to do something great in your life and great for your family. Maybe no one in your immediate family ever went to college; you be the first to go and graduate! Or maybe none of your friends have a desire to leave home; you be the one to travel the world and come back to share all your stories with them. Some people close to you will never know what success looks like or believe that success can ever happen for their lives until they first see it happen in yours. Just like some of your peers who you walk the halls with you every day will never know what true love looks like until they see the love in you. To my students, understand this, you have everything inside of you right now to do anything big or small that you could possibly dream of but first you must believe that you can conquer ALL things.

My son Kyle Aubrey Greene, Jr. whom I affectionately call "KJ" is only nine (right now) but when he was eight he came to both his mother and me saying; "I want to launch my own t-shirt line." At first I thought he just wanted to piggyback off my #KyleSpeaks t-shirt clothing line but his idea of shirts had absolutely no relation to mine. This eight year old kid saw the success that I had in creating, producing, and selling my shirts and he believed that he could re-create that same success for himself. KJ decided to take ownership of his success in the present to position himself for true success in his future. Are you still renting your success to someone else? When will you decide to OWN IT?!?! When he released his first basketball themed shirt, "My Game is Wet" (a basketball swooshing through a basket) he experienced instant success. His first print sold out amongst friends and family. KJ also has his own website (www.atrueballer.com) which he helped to create and design (with his mother's Charmane help) where he sells his shirts. Where are all my other students with a dream and some goals? Who is ready to unlock their future success right now in their present? You can start becoming great right now and it will help propel you to greatness down the road. KJ decided that he didn't want to wait until after high school or college to do something great in his life. He figured he could get the ball rolling in elementary school. Students, what are you waiting on? Do you have a desire to want more out of your life? Have you seen your parents struggle long enough and come to the realization that you don't want to struggle like your mother or your father. I loved my grandmother enough growing up and watching her cry as she struggled in deciding if she'd pay the light bill or buy her medicine that it made me realize that I didn't want to endure those same types of struggles. Let your personal struggles or the struggles of loved ones become your inner motivation. Let it be the fuel to your fire. Do not just look to this book alone for motivation. I believe that if each of you were to reach deep down inside, you would unlock a new level of creativity, a new level of importance, a new level significance, a new level of imagination, a new level of confidence, a new level of hope, and a new level of greatness that you did not know existed in you.

1. What do you believe your roles are as a student?
2. Do you seek and apply advice from your parent(s) and elders?
3. If your parent(s) are not around, do you have a mentor or someone who you can talk to for guidance?
4. Are you walking towards greatness?
5. Will you choose today to take ownership of your success?

S.T.U.D.E.N.T = A person that **Succeeds Through Unique Dares Endlessly and Nobly Tough**

I dare each student reading this chapter to go out and tackle the world. I dare you to defy all the odds that may have been stacked against you or said about you. Who cares if you had a mother on drugs or a father in prison? You do not become that same type of parent one day. I dare you to lead the crowd and to not just become the next follower. I dare you to dream the BIGGEST dream. But I double dare you to make your biggest dream the world's greatest REALITY!

Journey Reflections

Students: You Are the Future

Bonus: Journey 19

Parents: Your Student Needs You

The one role that you cannot take for granted in today's society is the role that YOU play in YOUR child's life. Their future success or failure depends on what you impart inside of them today.

1. What do you believe your role is as a parent?
2. Do you feel like you parent effectively?

Have you ever, like me, awoke one morning and sat on the edge saying to yourself, "I don't want to adult today; please don't make me adult." Then you quickly realize, as your screaming child bursts into the room, that that option is no longer a viable one. Our children are our world but they also are responsible for changing our world drastically as we once knew it. As parents it quickly becomes our responsibility to give our kids everything that they need (from time, love, resources, attention, to skills etc.) in order to be successful in life. But the responsibility also lies upon us to try and keep everything away from them (from negative influences, bad situations, to wicked people etc.) that could compromise their future success. I actually had to learn all of this the hard way and in a hurry. As a result of my actions, I grew up quicker than I had hoped and I discovered what it meant to be an adult instantly. For I had a child when I was still just a child myself. I had my daughter at the tender age of sixteen while I was in the tenth grade. Can you say, "Reality check?" But check this, I flipped the script and instead of using my daughter as an excuse to stop or to look at my own life as a failure; I chose to use my daughter as my motivation and my reason to never stop and to never give up. A potential excuse suddenly became my internal rallying cry for self-motivation. A failure quickly taught me what it meant to trust my faith. I went from 0 to 100 real quick (in my Drake voice). Literally! I went from seeing myself as a failure to realizing that I was not a failure because I had failed, but that now I had an opportunity to become a great father if only I tried. I went from being a carefree teenager with absolutely no responsibilities to a very young and scared father with now so many responsibilities before him. I went from a student only needing to worry about school stuff like grades and sports to a parent constantly worrying about real life issues like being able to afford diapers and milk for my child. I often found myself wondering, "How am I going to be able to take care of this child when I can't even take care of myself." Parents, have you ever been in a dark place where you were not sure how you were going to make it? At that point in your life when adversity strikes and you find yourself down for the count, you must always stand strong in the batter's box ready to swing at the next best pitch--your next best opportunity. Here is where you must not panic thinking you need a home run to win the game because all you need is a hit to get in scoring position. Parents, when your situation gets tight and your money starts to look funny, do not panic or simply give up because one swing, one word, one opportunity, or one yes can change your life as you once knew it. I want to talk about the challenges that a 21st century parent faces and the mindset that one must have to overcome those challenges.

As a parent you quickly realize that your life choices no longer affect just you; they affect another human being and one who is closer to you than anyone else. Your child is immediately and directly impacted by every choice (good or bad) that you make in your life. I had friends while in high school that experimented with drugs and alcohol, so whenever I wanted to hang out with them I had to create a strong enough mindset of not being easily persuaded into doing something that could jeopardize both me and my child. So whenever a blunt got passed around, I had to have enough mental fortitude and will power to say, "Nah, I'm good, I pass. I can't do that because I've got a daughter now." And after a while they saw that I was not moving away from this position and they eventually respected it. We used to have the most fun at our high school dances and some nights when we were able to get inside a club we did, but I knew that I could not drink because had I gotten too drunk, it could result in me being in a very bad accident. And I did not want my daughter to grown up fatherless. So, as parents we immediately realize that it is no longer about us but it is now all about our child; the one that looks into our eyes with a smile of hope and trust. The one that grabs a hold of our finger are instantly become comforted by our warm touch. We protect them with the same vigor as our military protects our freedom. We know without even saying that their future is riding directly on us and on the choices that we make for them. As parents we accept the reality that no one gives out manuals on how to be a successful parent but we must learn (many times through trial and error) how to parent successfully and strategically for the sake of our children. So we must create a new mindset on how we parent, especially if is our true desire to give our children the type of life that we may have never experienced. I always said to myself that I wanted to give my kids a life (when I was growing up) that I did not think was possible. I want to give them the things in life that I always thought were impossible. Parents let me let you in on a little secret, your child will never be great in life if you are not willing to do some great things towards their process in discovering their greatness. When I say, "great things" I simply mean great things like spending time with them, showing them that you care by your actions, investing valuable resources and trainings for their future and showing them why sometimes (paraphrasing Robert Frost's great poem) taking the road less traveled could make the greatest difference in their life. I personally believe that 21st century parents can no longer parent like those from the 19th century. Please understand this is not a knock or any shade thrown onto the parents from that time because many children from that era (I feel) had more respect for not just their elders but more importantly for themselves. Children back then did not have as many distractions that plague our kids today. I am a '80's baby who graduated high school in the year of 2000 (Y2K remember that) without having a cellphone, Facebook, Twitter, Snap-Chat, Instagram, FaceTime, Kik, or Skype. Can you believe that? MySpace and BlackPlanet had not even been created yet. Heck, there were only a few students in my high school who I was aware of who had pagers/beepers or the huge cellphones. But yet, we made it! We survived with much fewer interferences than those that haunt our children today. I spoke about having my daughter at 16 who is now 17, but I have a 9 year old son. KJ (Kyle Jr.) has an iPhone (I don't even have an iPhone), a tablet, every gaming system from a Wii to an xBox1, he only has an Instagram and SnapChat account, but the fact yet remains he is ONLY 9. Parents, when you believe that outside forces are interrupting or disturbing the focus of your child, it is your job to remove those interruptions. My daughter slipped on her grades one time; I took her cellphone, took her off the track team and when I discovered she was accessing her social media sites on her tablet I took that too. Her grades over the course of that semester improved tremendously and she earned back everything that she had lost earlier in the semester. The 21st century parent must be mentally dope! You have to be a dope parent and then know when to parent as a dope friend. I use to hear people say, "I'm NOT my child's friend." You are entitled to your own opinion, but when I say this I say it from my own two case studies (my two kids). I am their best friend and as a result they share with me their most intimate problems. Do NOT lose your child or your children to a friend in the streets when they yearned to have a friendship with you. I speak to kids all over from elementary, middle, high, charter, alternative schools, DJJ (Department of Juvenile Justice), non-profit organizations, and churches that share with me the issues that haunt them. I hear time and time again, "Mr. Kyle my mother and I don't have a good relationship. I can't even talk to her; it's like she doesn't even care." Or some of the young men say, "Mr. Kyle I just want my father to be involved in my life." We as parents have to be there for our children in every aspect of their lives. If I have to be the judge, I'll do it! If I have to be the doctor because they're hurt, I'll do it! If they need an ear to talk into or a shoulder to cry on, I give them mine. We live in a world where people prey on the inactions of parents when they are looking to gain the trust from your child. Do NOT give them the satisfaction of controlling your child actions.

In other words, I believe that parents can no longer just coach from the sidelines. Parents, if you want to be effective, you must come down from your perch of comfort and you must be willing to get a little dirty. You will get a little dirty by injecting yourself into your child's world. Your child will appreciate your hands-on approach because children realize that there will come a time when they want to do what they were taught. There will come a point in your child's life where you must coach from the press box because you have to allow them the chance to call the right play and to then execute it out to the best of their abilities. However, this execution directly depends on how well you prepared them during practice. And hopefully during practice you were hands-on enough to show them the correct fundamentals of the process. This process could be anything from how to clean the house correctly, how to drive a car properly or how to balance a checkbook effectively. But just make sure you do your part as a parent to instill within them the correct fundamentals. I parent the same way I coach basketball. I will never just tell a basketball player that I coach or train what I want done in a drill or in a game without first illustrating it for them. My belief is simple: if you see me do it, you can then see yourself doing it. I actually learn better that way because you can tell me how to do something until you're blue in the face and I still might not get it, but if you show me how to do something I can retain that teaching more efficiently.

Parents do NOT be afraid of being your child's best teacher of life principles. What you teach them today they will be able to apply for a lifetime. As a 21st century parent we have to go the extra step to instill inside our children what not giving up looks like. When our days get tough we have to show our children what getting tougher looks like. Because one day, they will look back over their lives as a parent and they will thank you for always being there for them as they are now there for their children.

1. How has this chapter helped you in your mentality as a parent in the 21st century?
2. What can you change right now to become more effective?
3. Have you ever looked back over your life and thanked your parents for the values that they instilled in you?
4. If not, don't let another day pass you by without thanking them.

Journey Reflections

The Journey Ends...

YOU DID IT! Congratulations you have made it to the end. I pray that The Mentality Changer was able to help change how you once thought about you. Our journey together comes to an end but your journey in life yet remains. Go out and do something great in your life. I believe that your greatest moments are ahead of you. No more waiting. Hopefully, you will begin to dance in the rain because you now realize that tough times don't last always but tough people do! Please be encouraged knowing that a minor setback is only a setup for a major comeback! You are a stronger person today as a result of reading this book and let me say again, "THANK YOU!"

Closing RULES:

- Share your review of The Mentality Changer on Social Media.
- Use the hashtag #TheMentalityChanger
- Share your journey with a friend.
- Encourage someone to start their journey today.

DARE to DREAM! DREAM to DO! DO to LIVE!

The Journey Ends

For more information about having Kyle A. Greene speak at your next event, to find out where his next live event will be held, or to get free updates, tips, and videos, please go to www.kyleagreene.com

About the Author

Kyle Aubrey Greene was born in Savannah, Georgia but raised on the outskirts of Ridgeland, South Carolina in a small community called "Pineland." Kyle will tell anyone who will listen that Pineland got its name because so many "pine" trees could be found on so much of "land" there; so... Pine + Land = Pineland. He was raised by his elderly grandmother, a woman who he believes passed on to him her very giving spirit and her huge loving heart. Kyle was educated in the Jasper County School District where he excelled in the classroom, on the basketball court, on the football field, and in track. Academics and sports were the vehicles which he used to help navigate him through high school and into college where he was awarded both academic and athletic scholarships. There too Kyle excelled in the classroom, on the football field, and in track. He graduated from Benedict College (cum laude) in 2004 with his Bachelor's degree in Computer Information Science. While at Benedict College, he learned a valuable lesson on serving because in order to graduate each student had to complete at least 120 hours of community service. Serving other people less fortunate than yourself... A national event occurred and it stirred something within Kyle to serve his local community, and he did. As a result of him giving of himself and serving others he would be propelled to his purpose in life. Kyle Greene the founder of #KyleSpeaks speaks all over the Southeast helping people to change their mindsets, helping people to discover their purpose in life, and helping people to overcome failures by passionately sharing how he overcame his. Kyle has been a guest on both Fox News Sean Hannity show and CBN 700 Club. He has been recognized in South Carolina as being One of the Most Interesting Minorities in 2013 (Minority Eye) and inducted into the first South Carolina Black Pages "Top 40 Under 40" (at the age of 32). There is nothing greater to Kyle's heart than his ability to touch, help, and impact another person's life.